Index

Deal 1

Defence is often regarded as the most difficult part of the game, although you get twice as much time to practice than declaring (half the time you are on the declaring side you are dummy).

Defenders start life more in the dark than declarer. The play of their first card is without a sight of dummy *(see Opening Lead book)*; they are unable accurately to assess their combined assets, counting winners and losers.

However the defenders do have one big advantage: they are two heads against one. To benefit fully from their two heads, it is vital that they function properly as a partnership, signalling information effectively to one another.

This Book will outline simple methods by which the defenders can convey their wishes to partner. No nodding, no winking, no slapping cards on the table, you understand. Signalling refers purely to the card played; it must be done demurely, in the same tempo and manner as any other card.

Communicating your defensive wishes to partner is a fascinating challenge, and one that has moved on a long way in recent decades. The old "Don't signal to me, let's keep declarer (as well as myself) in the dark" approach has been replaced by a much more cooperative style. I look forward to illuminating you, as the defenders are able to illuminate each other.

By far the most important signal, as we shall see, is the "Attitude Signal", in which you tell partner whether you would like him to continue the suit he has led.

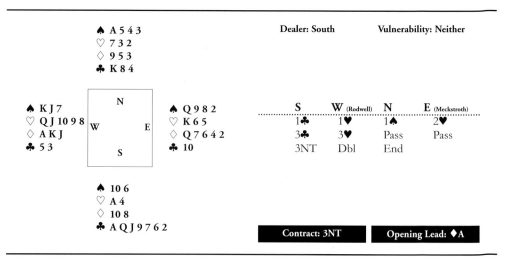

	Dealer: South		**Vulnerability: Neither**		

S	W (Rodwell)	N	E (Meckstroth)
1♣	1♥	1♠	2♥
3♣	3♥	Pass	Pass
3NT	Dbl	End	

Contract: 3NT **Opening Lead: ♦A**

Our first deal in the series sees USA's top pair Meckstroth-Rodwell in action, in the famous 1992 Naturalist-Scientist Match in London, in which the Naturals - I was one - were allowed no bidding conventions. [We lost, but it was generally accepted that we were defeated more because of inferior play, than our lack of bidding weaponry].

South's 3NT gamble would have succeeded on a heart lead or switch - with seven club tricks and the two major-suit aces. But West led the ace of diamonds - to have a look at dummy and receive a signal from partner. When partner threw an encouraging high card (the seven), he continued with the king, then jack. East overtook with the queen and cashed his two remaining spot cards. Down one.

Deal 2

Here are some of the things you can say to partner when signalling in defence,

"Please try another suit".

"Please lead a spade".

"I have an even number of diamonds".

"I want a ruff".

"I like the suit you led".

"I want to stop playing Bridge and take the dog for a walk" (only kidding).

The range of possibilities is seemingly almost endless, but one basic point must be made clear: You only convey one message with one card. In other words you can say "Please try another suit" in one situation; and "I have an even number of diamonds" in another. However you cannot send both these messages at once. Therefore it is clearly vital for partner to know what your signal means.

As you would expect in a game so logical as Bridge, signals have evolved such that partner receives what rates to be the most important piece of information in a given situation.

Say partner leads the ace of a suit.

Question: What is he most likely to want to know?

Answer: Whether you would like him to continue that suit.

Telling partner your attitude towards the suit he has led is the most important signal of all, known, appropriately, as the "Attitude Signal". Our second deal sees this "Like/Dislike" signal play a crucial role.

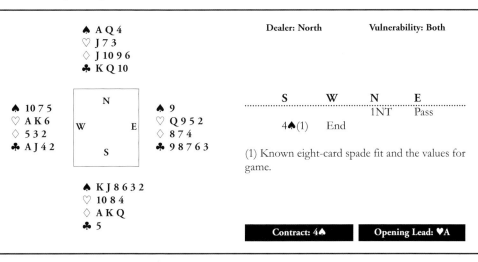

	♠ A Q 4		
	♡ J 7 3		
	◇ J 10 9 6		
	♣ K Q 10		

Dealer: North **Vulnerability: Both**

West
♠ 10 7 5
♡ A K 6
◇ 5 3 2
♣ A J 4 2

East
♠ 9
♡ Q 9 5 2
◇ 8 7 4
♣ 9 8 7 6 3

South
♠ K J 8 6 3 2
♡ 10 8 4
◇ A K Q
♣ 5

S	W	N	E
		1NT	Pass
4♠(1)	End		

(1) Known eight-card spade fit and the values for game.

| **Contract: 4♠** | **Opening Lead: ♥A** |

West led the ace of hearts to 4♠. One reason why ace from ace-king is the best type of lead against a trump contract is that partner is able to signal to tell you whether or not to continue the suit. Here, East signalled with the nine.

This high spot card was a request for West to continue the suit. West led out the king of hearts at Trick Two, and was just about to lead a third heart to his partner's presumed queen, when he reflected that his partner might not know what to do next. West therefore cleverly cashed the ace of clubs at Trick Three (key play), and only then led a third heart to his partner's queen. Down one.

Note that if West does not cash his ace of clubs, and East returns a diamond (the natural-looking play given dummy's cards), declarer would dispose of his club on the fourth diamond, and make his game.

Deal 3

Question: What is a signal?

Answer: It is a defensive card that is not played to contribute to the winning of the actual trick. Rather, it is made to convey a message to partner.

The most important type of signal, by far, is the like/dislike, or "Attitude" Signal. By playing an unnecessarily high card (e.g. an eight), you are saying that you want partner to continue the suit he has led. Playing your lowest card has the opposite meaning.

> ***"Throw high means aye***
> ***Throw low means no".***

Various issues relating to this Attitude Signal must be addressed, including:

(i) When is my card a signal?

(ii) When should I encourage (throw high), and when should I discourage (throw low)?

(iii) What is "high", and what is "low"?

We will consider these (and other) issues in more detail, but the simple answers to the above are:

(i) Your card is an Attitude Signal when partner has led, on the first round of a suit, and you cannot contribute to the winning of the trick.

(ii) You should encourage when you have an equal honour to the honour partner led, or can trump ("ruff"), or (more subtly) do not want partner to switch suits.

(iii) It is all relative, not absolute. If partner leads an ace (from ace-king), you will have to play the three from Q32, yet the seven from 987. Partner will have to scrutinise the other spot cards in order to interpret the signal accurately - take this deal.

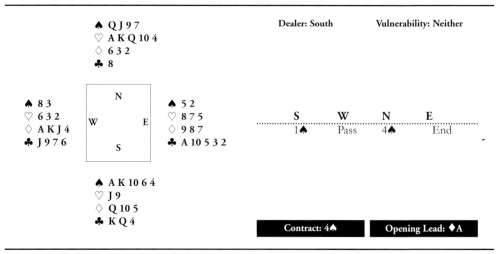

```
              ♠ Q J 9 7
              ♡ A K Q 10 4
              ♢ 6 3 2
              ♣ 8
                    N
  ♠ 8 3                        ♠ 5 2
  ♡ 6 3 2     W         E      ♡ 8 7 5
  ♢ A K J 4                    ♢ 9 8 7
  ♣ J 9 7 6        S           ♣ A 10 5 3 2

              ♠ A K 10 6 4
              ♡ J 9
              ♢ Q 10 5
              ♣ K Q 4
```

Dealer: South   **Vulnerability: Neither**

S	W	N	E
1♠	Pass	4♠	End

Contract: 4♠   **Opening Lead: ♦A**

West led the ace of diamonds against 4♠. Dummy played the two, East the seven, and declarer the five. The seven looked like a "throw high means aye - yes please" signal. Or was it?

West looked closely at the diamond spot cards. Dummy held the two, three and six; he, himself, held the four, and declarer followed to Trick One with the five. The seven was partner's lowest card!

West now knew not to continue with the king of diamonds, as it would promote declarer's queen. Instead he switched to a club (he could hardly switch to hearts, looking at dummy). East won the ace, and a second diamond lead, crucially through declarer's queen-ten, ensured that West scored both his king-jack. He beat declarer's ten with the jack, and cashed the king, felling his queen. Down one.

Deal 4

Question: When is your card a signal?

Answer: When, on the first round of a suit, you are not contributing to the winning of the trick.

E.g.

Partner	*Dummy* ♠A85	*You*
leads ♠2		(i) ♠K94
		(ii) ♠1073

If dummy plays low, you must play, in (i), the king, in order to win the trick; in (ii) the ten, in order to force out a higher card from declarer. These are not signals.

However if dummy plays the ace, you cannot contribute to the trick in any way. That means that your card is a signal to partner. In (i) you play the nine; in (ii) the three. You do this to conform to the Attitude Signal ditty:

> **"Throw high means aye**
> **Throw low means no".**

[Contrast this with leading, where the ditty is: Lead Low for Like, Lead High for Hate.]

What would you signal in the following situations?

Partner	*Dummy* ♥853	*You*
leads ♥A		(i) ♥Q92
		(ii) ♥J92

(i) Assuming that partner is leading ace from ace-king, your queen is an "equal honour". You should encourage partner to continue, by playing the nine.

(ii) The jack is not a significant enough high card - it is not equal to the ace-king. Take this layout:

$$♥853$$
$$♥AK104 \qquad ♥J92$$
$$♥Q76$$

Declarer will not make a trick with his queen - unless West continues with the king. To prevent him from doing so, East plays a discouraging two.

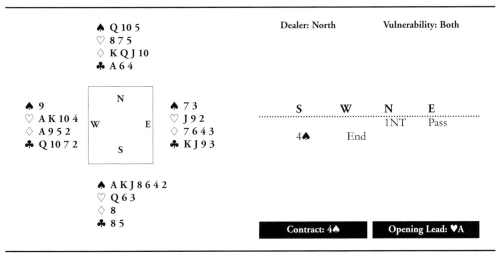

	♠ Q 10 5	
	♡ 8 7 5	
	◇ K Q J 10	
	♣ A 6 4	

♠ 9		♠ 7 3
♡ A K 10 4	W E	♡ J 9 2
◇ A 9 5 2		◇ 7 6 4 3
♣ Q 10 7 2		♣ K J 9 3

	♠ A K J 8 6 4 2	
	♡ Q 6 3	
	◇ 8	
	♣ 8 5	

Dealer: North **Vulnerability: Both**

S	W	N	E
		1NT	Pass
4♠	End		

Contract: 4♠	**Opening Lead: ♥A**

West leads the ace of hearts against 4♠, and East correctly signals with the two ("throw low means no"). With the threat of dummy's diamonds, West correctly shifts to the two of clubs. Declarer rises with dummy's ace, and East has the opportunity for a second signal. This time, liking clubs, he follows with the nine ("throw high means aye").

After drawing trumps, declarer leads a diamond. But West grabs his ace (in case of the actuality - declarer has a singleton), and leads a second club. East wins the king then a heart lead, crucially through declarer's queen, sees West beat the queen with the king. The defence score the third round, and that means down two.

Deal 5

Partner leads an ace (from ace-king) at Trick One to a suit contract.

Question: When should you encourage partner's ace-lead?

Answer: When you have third-round control: the queen, or a doubleton (and can ruff).

The above guide - resulting in ace, king and a third round - will backfire if declarer holds just two cards. To work out the likelihood of him holding just a doubleton, the best approach, with no other information, is to guess that partner's ace-lead is from ace-king-small-small (four cards), and then work out, and base your signal, on whether declarer has a third card.

E.g.

		Dummy	
		(a) ♦J108	
Partner		(b) ♦J1085	*You*
leads ♦A			(i) ♦Q94
			(ii) ♦94

(a)(i). Encourage with the nine. Giving partner ♦AKxx leaves declarer with ♦xxx.

(a)(ii). Encourage with the nine. You are ruffing the third round.

(b)(i). Discourage with the four. There is too great a chance that declarer is short, and that ace, king, over-to-the-queen will see declarer ruff, and later throw a loser on dummy's promoted fourth-round winner.

(b)(ii). Encourage with the nine. You can ruff the third round

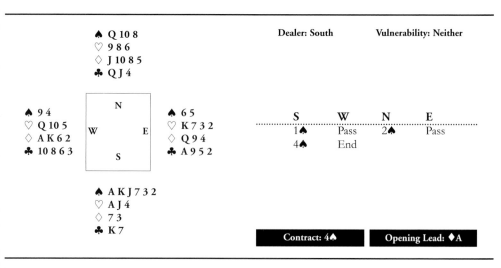

♠ Q 10 8
♡ 9 8 6
♢ J 10 8 5
♣ Q J 4

♠ 9 4
♡ Q 10 5
♢ A K 6 2
♣ 10 8 6 3

N
W E
S

♠ 6 5
♡ K 7 3 2
♢ Q 9 4
♣ A 9 5 2

♠ A K J 7 3 2
♡ A J 4
♢ 7 3
♣ K 7

Dealer: South　　**Vulnerability: Neither**

S	W	N	E
1♠	Pass	2♠	Pass
4♠	End		

Contract: 4♠　　**Opening Lead: ♦A**

West leads the ace of diamonds against 4♠. Over to East - where a casual encouraging signal of the nine ("throw high means aye") would be fatal.

West would unwittingly play king and a third diamond, hoping (expecting) for East to trump. In fact it would be declarer who trumps. Trumps can be drawn in two rounds (leaving a dummy entry with the third trump), the ace of clubs forced out, and declarer's two heart losers going on the promoted fourth diamond and third club. Game made.

Discourage West's ace of diamonds lead, as East at Trick One, and West will (looking at dummy's weakness) switch to a low heart (to your king and declarer's ace). Declarer draws trumps and leads the king of clubs, but you win the ace and return a second heart. West scores both his queen-ten, plus the king of diamonds, and that makes five defensive tricks. Down two.

Deal 6

"Hilo" signals and doubletons are often associated with one another. This may be right with leads - you should always lead the high card from a doubleton. However it is a dangerous association for signals.

You should not always give the "hi-lo" (i.e. high-then-low) signal when following suit to partner's lead. There is nothing magical about the doubleton holding that merits an automatic hi-lo. Only play hi-lo if you genuinely want partner to continue with his lead; in other words if you want him to give you a third-round ruff.

Here are some scenarios where it would be a mistake to signal high with a doubleton:
(i) It is notrumps.
(ii) You have no trumps.
(iii) You do not want a ruff, because it would be at the cost of a natural trump trick (e.g QJ10).

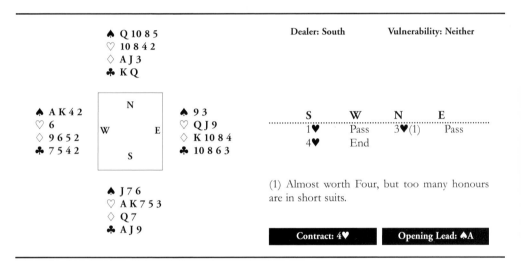

Dealer: South   **Vulnerability: Neither**

S	W	N	E
1♥	Pass	3♥(1)	Pass
4♥	End		

(1) Almost worth Four, but too many honours are in short suits.

Contract: 4♥   **Opening Lead: ♠A**

West led the ace of spades against 4♥, and East had to decide what to signal. What is it to be: "Throw high means aye", or "throw low means no"?

Correctly rejecting the reflex hi-lo for a doubleton, East reflected that he did not want a spade ruff, because it would be at the cost of his natural trump trick. Receiving his spade ruff would set up a spade winner in dummy, on which declarer would discard a diamond loser from hand. Declarer would thus make his game, losing just the first three tricks.

East did not signal with the nine of spades at Trick One, but rather with the three ("throw low means no"). Key play. West switched to a diamond at Trick Two (clearly best looking at dummy, trying set to set up a slow trick for his partner), and declarer was now sunk.

Hoping (his only chance) for West to hold the king of diamonds, declarer played low from dummy. No good - East won the king, and reverted back to spades (knowing West that held the king for his lead of the ace). West won his king, and East's trump holding had to score the setting trick, whether or not West led a third spade for East to ruff. Down one.

Deal 7

Partner leads an ace (from ace-king). Provided dummy's holding makes it likely that three rounds of the suit will stand up, you should encourage when:

      (a) You have the queen, or

      (b) You have a doubleton.

Catering to both possibilities, partner will then follow up with the king and a third round. You will then either (a) win your queen, or (b) ruff.

It is important to stress, however, that it must not be a reflex reaction to signal high from a doubleton (unlike a lead - which should always be top from two).

Here are some situations in which it is incorrect to encourage (by playing the higher card) holding a doubleton:

(i) It is notrumps.

(ii) You have no trumps.

(iii) You do not want a ruff, because it would be at the cost of a natural trump trick (e.g QJ10).

(iv) Dummy has length (typically five cards), so that declarer rates to be short.

(v) You have Qx.

Let us consider point (v) in more detail. Normal practice is to encourage with the higher card from a doubleton when holding anything from 32 up to J2, but to refrain from playing the queen from Q2 (it is too valuable a card).

There is a useful corollary to withholding the queen from queen-small: the play of the queen should show either (a) the jack as well, or (b) a singleton. In either case a second-round underlead of the king from partner will see you (a) win the jack, or (b) ruff.

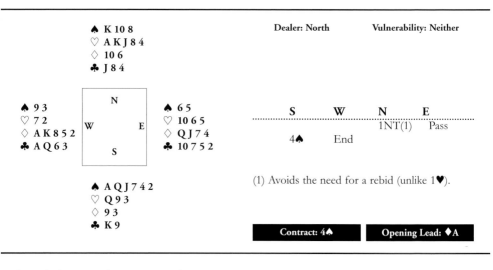

| | | | | Dealer: North | Vulnerability: Neither |

North
♠ K 10 8
♡ A K J 8 4
◇ 10 6
♣ J 8 4

West
♠ 9 3
♡ 7 2
◇ A K 8 5 2
♣ A Q 6 3

East
♠ 6 5
♡ 10 6 5
◇ Q J 7 4
♣ 10 7 5 2

South
♠ A Q J 7 4 2
♡ Q 9 3
◇ 9 3
♣ K 9

S	W	N	E
		1NT(1)	Pass
4♠	End		

(1) Avoids the need for a rebid (unlike 1♥).

| Contract: 4♠ | Opening Lead: ◆A |

This deal sees the power of such an underlead. West led the ace of diamonds against 4♠, and East correctly played the queen. He did not know whether he wanted his partner to underlead his king at Trick Two, but it cost nothing to advertise the jack (or a singleton - unlikely here).

West was desperate to put his partner on play - for a club lead through declarer's putative king. He took advantage of his partner's cooperative queen-signal, and led a low diamond at Trick Two.

East won the jack of diamonds, and duly returned a club - looking at dummy's weakness. West could now score both his queen of clubs (declarer guessed to play low from hand - in a lose-lose position), and then cash the ace (felling declarer's king). Down one - the only winning defence.

Deal 8

When not aiming for a third-round ruff (holding a doubleton), you will encourage partner's honour lead when you hold an equal honour.

If partner leads an ace (from ace-king), the equal honour is the queen; when partner leads a king (from king-queen), there are two equal honours: the ace and the jack.

E.g.

Dummy
♣ 752

Partner
leads ♣K

You
(i) ♣A<u>9</u>4
(ii) ♣<u>J</u>94
(iii)♣109<u>4</u>

Signal with the underlined card in each case.

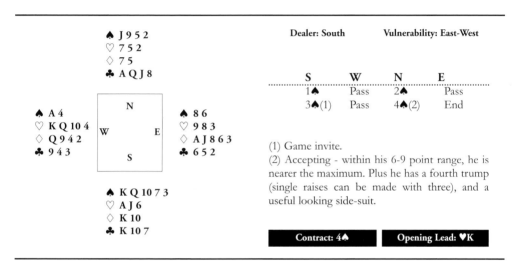

♠ J 9 5 2
♡ 7 5 2
◇ 7 5
♣ A Q J 8

♠ A 4
♡ K Q 10 4
◇ Q 9 4 2
♣ 9 4 3

♠ 8 6
♡ 9 8 3
◇ A J 8 6 3
♣ 6 5 2

♠ K Q 10 7 3
♡ A J 6
◇ K 10
♣ K 10 7

Dealer: South   **Vulnerability: East-West**

S	W	N	E
1♠	Pass	2♠	Pass
3♠(1)	Pass	4♠(2)	End

(1) Game invite.
(2) Accepting - within his 6-9 point range, he is nearer the maximum. Plus he has a fourth trump (single raises can be made with three), and a useful looking side-suit.

Contract: 4♠   **Opening Lead: ♥K**

West leads the king of hearts against 4♠. When East correctly signals with the three ("throw low means no"), West knows that declarer holds both the ace and the jack. Declarer has to decide whether or not to win his ace, and we will consider both variants:

(A) Declarer wins the ace of hearts at Trick One. He then leads the king of trumps. West wins the ace, and does not cash the promoted queen of hearts, for he knows that it will set up declarer's jack (unless it is singleton). Instead he switches to a diamond (dummy's weakness). East wins his ace and reverts to hearts, crucially leading through declarer's jack. Not only does West score his queen, he also scores his ten. Down one.

(B) Declarer ducks Trick One, letting West hold the king of hearts. West knows - from East's "throw low means no" signal of the three of hearts - that a second heart lead will be into declarer's ace-jack. He therefore switches to a diamond (dummy's weakness). East wins the ace and a second heart, crucially through declarer's ace-jack, seals declarer's fate. He can do no better than rise with the ace, and lead the king of trumps. But West takes his ace, and follows with the queen of hearts. Down one.

Note that on other defences, declarer can discard a heart on dummy's fourth club (after drawing trumps). Game made.

Deal 9

Unless short and desiring a ruff, you should plan to signal encouragement for partner's honour lead ("throw high means aye") when you have an equal honour.

Partner's Lead	Equal Honour(s)
Ace (from ace-king)	Queen
King (from king-queen)	Ace, Jack
Queen (from queen-jack)	King, ten

Encouraging partner's lead when holding a mere ten in the suit seems far from obvious. However when partner leads the queen (showing the jack), the ten is an equal honour. Provided a look at dummy's holding suggests that three rounds of the suit will stand up, the encouraging signal can be essential.

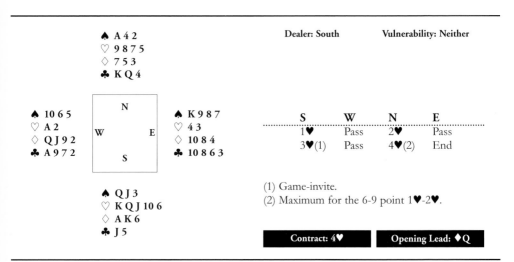

```
                 ♠ A 4 2
                 ♡ 9 8 7 5
                 ◇ 7 5 3
                 ♣ K Q 4
   ♠ 10 6 5         N          ♠ K 9 8 7
   ♡ A 2                       ♡ 4 3
   ◇ Q J 9 2   W       E       ◇ 10 8 4
   ♣ A 9 7 2                   ♣ 10 8 6 3
                   S
                 ♠ Q J 3
                 ♡ K Q J 10 6
                 ◇ A K 6
                 ♣ J 5
```

Dealer: South   Vulnerability: Neither

S	W	N	E
1♥	Pass	2♥	Pass
3♥(1)	Pass	4♥(2)	End

(1) Game-invite.
(2) Maximum for the 6-9 point 1♥-2♥.

Contract: 4♥   **Opening Lead: ◆Q**

West led the queen of diamonds against the 4♥ game, and, holding the equal honour, the ten, East correctly signalled with the eight ("throw high means aye"). Declarer won the king, and led the king of trumps (was that the right play?).

Winning his ace of trumps, West now knew to lead a second (low) diamond, knowing declarer did not hold ◆AK10. East played his crucial ten, forcing out declarer's ace.

Declarer could not make his game any longer. He drew trumps and ran the queen of spades, but East won the king, and led a third diamond over to his partner's promoted jack. West cashed the ace of clubs, and that meant down one.

Could declarer have done better - in spite of the efficient signalling? The answer is yes.

After winning Trick One with the king of diamonds, declarer needs to force out the ace of clubs. This will set up two club winners; on the second of these, he can discard his small diamond.

Lead the jack of clubs at Trick Two (key play). West does best to duck his ace, winning it when declarer next leads a second club. He leads a second diamond to East's ten and declarer's ace, and now declarer needs to cross to dummy to enjoy the club winner.

Declarer crosses to the ace of spades (no finesse), discards his small diamond on the promoted club, and only then plays on trumps. All the defence score are the aces of clubs and trumps, plus the king of spades. Game made.

Deal 10

The most important signal is the Attitude, or "Come-on" Signal. This tells you whether or nor partner would like you to continue the suit you have led. The motto is:

> "Throw high means aye
> Throw low means no".

Question: What is "high" and what is "low"?.
Answer: It is all relative. Whilst a two, three and four are usually low; and a seven, eight or nine usually high, you must look at the spot cards to see whether all is what it appears.

Exercise: In both (i) and (ii), partner signals (on your ace lead) with the seven. Is he encouraging or discouraging:

In (i), partner's seven is clearly discouraging ("throw low means no"): there are no lower spot cards unaccounted for. Perhaps he holds ♠987 or ♠J97.

In (ii), partner's seven is probably encouraging, for it appears that he also holds the three. Perhaps he holds ♠Q73 or ♠73. [It must be said, however, that a crafty declarer might be withholding the three, in order to scramble the signal (more on this anon).]

The moral is clear: you cannot merely look at the size of partner's card: you must scrutinise all the other visible spot cards too (in your hand, in dummy, and the card declarer played).

	Dummy	
You	♠1042	*Partner*
♠AK65		(i) ♠7
Lead ♠A	*Declarer*	(ii)♠7
	(i) ♠3	
	(ii) ♠8	

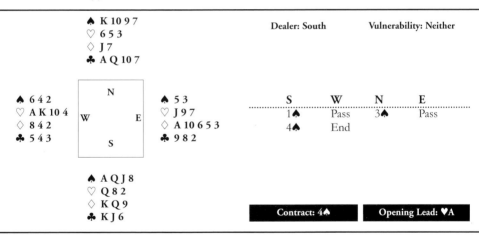

Dealer: South   Vulnerability: Neither

S	W	N	E
1♠	Pass	3♠	Pass
4♠	End		

Contract: 4♠   **Opening Lead: ♥A**

West led the ace of hearts against 4♠, and saw Trick One go ♥3, ♥7, ♥2. Although partner's seven looked high, closer scrutiny revealed that all the lower hearts were visible, therefore the seven was partner's lowest. Time for a switch.

It would be an error to switch to a club - if East holds the king of clubs he will always score the card (as you may have surmised, I intensely dislike the ditty "Lead through Strength"). Better (and essential here) to switch to dummy's weaker suit, diamonds.

East won Trick two with the ace of diamonds, and led a second heart, crucially through declarer's queen. West beat the queen with the king, and the defence scored the third round. Down one.

Footnote: had declarer followed to the first heart with the eight, might not West have thought that East held the two and was encouraging (from e.g. Q82)?

Deal 11

When declarer is leading a suit, it would be worse than pointless to signal your attitude. Who would benefit most? Right - declarer. However there is a potentially vital message you can give to partner: how many cards you hold in that suit, your "count".

By telling partner how many cards you hold in a suit, partner can work out how many cards declarer has in the suit; and that can be vital information. This will be particularly so in a situation in which dummy is entryless, and partner wants to win his ace on declarer's last card (to break the communications).

Here is the nub: with an even number of cards, you play high (a high spot card such as an eight or nine); with an odd number of cards, you play your lowest.

High-Even; Low-Odd: HELO

(A)   *Entryless Dummy*
  You   ♦KQJ106   *Partner*
  (i) ♦92   Has ♦A
  (ii)♦952
              Declarer
              Leads ♦3

Take (A): in (i) you play ♦9 (high-even); in (ii) you play ♦2 (low-odd). From this, partner can work out when to win his ♦A - (B) illustrates how:

(B)   *Entryless Dummy*
  You   ♦KQJ106   *Partner*
  (i) ♦9   ♦A74
  (ii)♦2   When to win?
              Declarer
              Leads ♦3

In (i), you have shown an even number of cards, presumably a doubleton (say declarer opened 1NT, so cannot have a singleton). That leaves declarer with three cards - partner now knows to win ♦A on the third round. In (ii) you have shown an odd number of cards (presumably three), leaving declarer with two. Partner will win his ace on the second round.

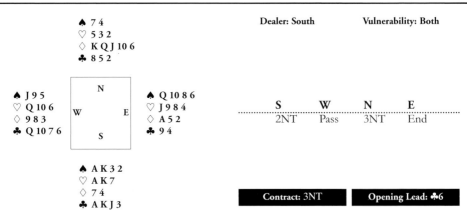

♠ 7 4		
♡ 5 3 2		
◇ K Q J 10 6		
♣ 8 5 2		

Dealer: South   **Vulnerability: Both**

♠ J 9 5
♡ Q 10 6
◇ 9 8 3
♣ Q 10 7 6

♠ Q 10 8 6
♡ J 9 8 4
◇ A 5 2
♣ 9 4

♠ A K 3 2
♡ A K 7
◇ 7 4
♣ A K J 3

S	W	N	E
2NT	Pass	3NT	End

Contract: 3NT   **Opening Lead: ♣6**

Declarer wins West's (unfortunate) club lead with his jack, and leads the four of diamonds, West following with the three (his lowest) to indicate an odd number (Low-Odd).

Presuming West for three diamonds, you as East can work out that declarer holds just two.

You therefore duck your ace once, winning it on the second round. With just one diamond trick, and no entry to return to dummy's established winners in the suit, declarer is held to eight tricks: ♠AK, ♥AK, ♣AKJ and one diamond. Down one.

Deal 12

By far the most important defensive signal is Attitude (like-dislike). When declarer is leading, however, the recommended signal is "Count".

The Count Signal

Showing partner how many cards you have in the suit led.

When?

Use when declarer leads a suit, and you think partner needs to know how many cards declarer holds. Typically this will be if partner needs to know when to take his ace (on declarer's last card).

Why?

Knowing how many cards partner holds in the suit tells you how many cards declarer holds.

How?

"HELO". HE stands for High-Even number; LO stands for Low-Odd number.

Telling partner how many cards you hold may be vital to partner; but declarer is also watching - take this slam deal.

	♠ Q J 9 3	
	♡ Q 5 2	
	◇ 7 4 2	
	♣ 9 8 5	

♠ 8 6 2		♠ A 7 4
♡ 10 8	N	♡ 9 7 4
◇ K 10 8 3	W E	◇ J 9 6 5
♣ J 10 7 6	S	♣ 4 3 2

	♠ K 10 5	
	♡ A K J 6 3	
	◇ A Q	
	♣ A K Q	

Dealer: South   **Vulnerability: Neither**

S	W	N	E
2♣(1)	Pass	2◇(2)	Pass
3NT(3)	Pass	4NT(4)	Pass
6♥(5)	Pass	Pass(6)	Pass

(1) 23+ points, or any game-force.
(2) Negative - up to eight points.
(3) 25-26 balanced, or maybe slightly more.
(4) (Very) optimistic notrump slam invite.
(5) Accepting the slam try, and offering his robust five-card suit as an alternative to 6NT.
(6) Opts for the eight-card heart fit, although 6NT would have proved easier.

Contract: 6♥   **Opening Lead: ♣J**

Declarer won West's club lead, and cashed the ace-jack of trumps, both following. If he used dummy's queen of trumps to draw the last outstanding trump, he would lack a dummy entry for the fourth spade, on the assumption that the defence would duck their ace until the third round. He would have to resort to the diamond finesse.

However when he led the king of spades out of his hand at Trick Four (best), West had to signal with the two, showing his odd number, so that East knew to delay winning his ace until the third round (he could work out declarer had three spades). Seeing the signal, and reading spades to split 3-3 as a result, declarer followed with the ten, not fearing the ruff that would ensue had the suit been splitting 4-2. East ducked again, and won a third spade with the ace.

There was no need for the diamond finesse any more. Declarer could rise with the ace on East's diamond return, cross to dummy's queen of trumps, then discard his queen of diamonds on dummy's fourth spade. 12 tricks and slam made.

Deal 13

The Count Signal (high=even number; low=odd number) is primarily used when declarer is leading a suit, and you think partner needs to know how many cards you (therefore declarer) hold. Typically, you suspect partner holds (say) the ace, and wishes to win it on declarer's last card. He can work out declarer's length if you show him your length.

"Giving the count" is vital in one or two other situations too. Say partner leads low, and you cannot beat dummy. Your attitude is now known, so showing count becomes the most useful information you can convey.

Exercise A: Which heart do you play after partner leads ♥5 and dummy plays ♥10?

	Dummy	
Partner	♥J104	*You*
Leads ♥5		(i) ♥862
		(ii) ♥73

Answers:
(i) ♥2 (low = odd number).
(ii) ♥7 (high = even)

Exercise B: Your ♥5 lead is won by dummy's ♥10. Work out declarer's original heart holding?

	Dummy	
You lead	♥J104	*Partner plays*
♥5 from		(i) ♥9
♥AQ752		(ii) ♥3

Answers:
(i) ♥Kxx. You need to put partner on play for a second heart lead through declarer's remaining ♥Kx.
(ii) ♥Kx. Declarer's ♥K is now singleton, and will fall under ♥A.

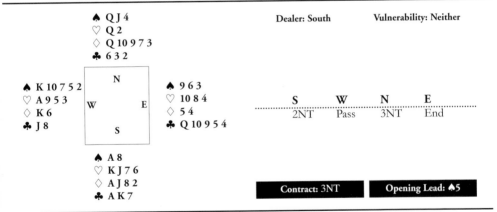

Dealer: South   Vulnerability: Neither

```
              ♠ Q J 4
              ♡ Q 2
              ◇ Q 10 9 7 3
              ♣ 6 3 2
♠ K 10 7 5 2      N      ♠ 9 6 3
♡ A 9 5 3    W     E     ♡ 10 8 4
◇ K 6                    ◇ 5 4
♣ J 8             S      ♣ Q 10 9 5 4
              ♠ A 8
              ♡ K J 7 6
              ◇ A J 8 2
              ♣ A K 7
```

S	W	N	E
2NT	Pass	3NT	End

| Contract: 3NT | Opening Lead: ♠5 |

West led the five of spades against 3NT, and declarer played dummy's jack. Because East could not beat dummy's card, his attitude was known (poor!). What was not known was the number of cards he held in the suit. This he showed by playing the three (low = odd).

West could now work out that, assuming the odd number was three - not one, declarer held just two spades. His ace was now bare. When at Trick Two declarer ran the ten of diamonds to his king, he was able to lead a low spade, safe in the knowledge that declarer's ace would "beat air".

After taking nothing with his ace, declarer ran his four diamond winners, but, needing a heart trick to bring his total to nine, tried the queen of hearts.

No good - West grabbed his ace and cashed the king of spades (felling dummy's queen) and followed with his two remaining small cards. Down one.

Deal 14

When my brother James and I started out in Bridge, venturing to our local Duplicate Club (Abingdon, Oxfordshire) as teenagers, we decided to give partner count in every suit (high=even; low=odd). This had the advantage that we could work out everybody's shape around the table, a terrific head-start when defending.

Unfortunately declarer was sometimes able to use the information to his/her advantage...

	Dummy	
Brother (1)	A1062	*Brother (2)*
J975		84
	Declarer	
	KQ3	

Brother (2) would play the eight-then-four on the king-queen, so declarer would know to finesse dummy's ten on the third round.

There are occasions in which giving count is vital. Not merely the classic position in which partner needs to know when to win an ace.

Take a situation in which partner has led and you cannot beat dummy's card (the jack or below). Normally you would give attitude on partner's lead, but if your attitude is known through your failure to contribute a high card to the trick, your count assumes most importance.

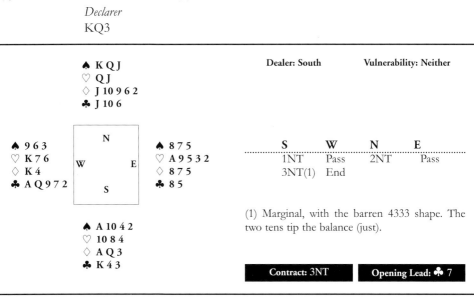

	S	W	N	E
	1NT	Pass	2NT	Pass
	3NT(1)	End		

Dealer: South   **Vulnerability: Neither**

(1) Marginal, with the barren 4333 shape. The two tens tip the balance (just).

Contract: 3NT	Opening Lead: ♣ 7

As West, you lead the seven of clubs to dummy's ten. Because East cannot beat dummy, and therefore his attitude (like/dislike) is known to be poor, he shows his count, playing the eight to show an even number (clearly two).

Declarer then leads and passes the jack of diamonds to your king. Knowing from partner's count signal that declarer has ♦Kx left, you need to put partner on play for a second club lead. He needs (and must have on the bidding) a major-suit ace. Which to lead?

Consider a wrong guess (for a right guess will end happily in either case). Leading a spade when partner holds the ace of hearts will be fatal - declarer having nine tricks in spades and diamonds; whereas leading a heart when partner holds the ace of spades will not - declarer still needs spade tricks to bring his total to nine.

You duly switch to a heart; East wins the ace, and a second club sees you score the ace-queen (felling the king), follow with two long clubs, and finally the king of hearts. Down three.

Deal 15

Think of Attitude as the primary defensive signal, and Count as the secondary one. The first round of a suit normally reveals your attitude (like/dislike), freeing up the second round card to show your count. It is normal to show your "present count"; in other words look to see how many cards you have left, and follow the normal Count Ditty: HELO (High = Even; Low = Odd).

Example (A):

Partner	Dummy ♣853	*You*
leads ♣AK		(i) ♣9742
		(ii) ♣972

In both (i) and (ii), you discourage on partner's ♣A by playing ♣2. If partner continues with ♣K anyway, then you can show your present count. In (i) you have a remaining odd number, so play low (♣4); in (ii) you have a remaining even number, so play high (♣9).

Example (B):

Partner	Dummy ♦A75	*You*
leads ♦4		(i) ♦K83
		(ii) ♦K932

Partner leads ♦4, to dummy's ♦5, and you win ♦K (in both examples). Say you elect to return a diamond (especially alluring in notrumps). In (i) you return ♦8, top of a remaining doubleton; in (ii) you return ♦2, low from a remaining odd number.

```
            ♠ 7 4
            ♡ J 6
            ♢ K Q 9 6
            ♣ A K J 9 6
                    N
♠ A 10 8 2              ♠ K J 3
♡ 9 8 5 3    W    E     ♡ A 10 7
♢ 10 5                  ♢ J 8 4 2
♣ 8 7 4          S      ♣ 5 3 2
            ♠ Q 9 6 5
            ♡ K Q 4 2
            ♢ A 7 3
            ♣ Q 10
```

Dealer: South   Vulnerability: Neither

S	W	N	E
1NT	Pass	3NT(1)	End

(1) No point in mentioning the minors. 3NT is almost bound to be easier than 5♣/♦.

Contract: 3NT   **Opening Lead: ♠2**

West led the two of spades against 3NT. East won the king, and correctly returned the jack, top of his remaining doubleton. Declarer covered with the queen, and West took his ace. What next?

If East had returned the three of spades, West would have known that the spade layout was:

```
            ♠74
♠A1082              ♠KJ63
            ♠Q95
```

and that four spade tricks could immediately be taken. As it was, West knew that he needed to put his partner back on play for a third spade lead through declarer's likely ♠9x.

Switching to dummy's weakest suit, hearts, West found his partner's ace, and East was able to lead the three of spades through declarer's nine, enabling West to score both his ♠108. Down one.

Deal 16

After you have shown partner your "Attitude" (i.e. "throw high means aye, throw low means no"), you can show him your "Count" (i.e. number of cards). Playing "Present Count" (recommended), you show him how many cards you have left, using HELO (High = Even; Low = Odd).

Exercise: You lead out ♥AK (versus a trump contract), and must decide whether ♥Q is cashing.

	Dummy ♥1063	
You ♥AKQ4		*Partner* (i) ♥2 then ♥5 (ii) ♥2 then ♥9
	Declarer ♥7 then ♥J	

Note: do not pay any attention to declarer's ♥J - it may easily be a (cost-nothing) false-card, with a lower heart still remaining.

In both (i) and (ii), partner discourages on ♥A. You now know that he cannot have a doubleton - or he would encourage (for a third-round ruff). You play ♥K.

In (i), partner follows with ♥5 - clearly his lowest. This indicates three remaining cards (HELO), therefore an initial four-card length; declarer must have started with a doubleton, and his ♥J is a true card. ♥Q is not cashing.

In (ii), partner's second-round ♥9 indicates a remaining even number (clearly a doubleton), therefore an initial three-card length; declarer must have started with three cards, and his ♥J is a false-card. Cash ♥Q.

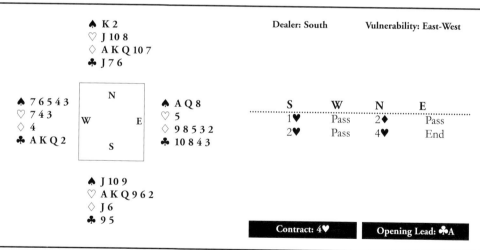

	S	W	N	E
	1♥	Pass	2♦	Pass
	2♥	Pass	4♥	End

Dealer: South **Vulnerability: East-West**

Contract: 4♥   **Opening Lead: ♣A**

West cashed the ace of clubs against 4♥, East signalling discouragement with the three. West followed with the king of clubs, East following with the four, and had to decide whether his queen would survive.

East's second club was his lowest, indicating a present odd number (presumably three), therefore an initial four-card length. This left declarer with an initial doubleton, and thus none left. West's queen was not cashing.

Although West started with the intention of switching to his singleton diamond, a glance at dummy made that unwise. It was surely better to switch to dummy's weaker suit, spades, and this West duly did.

With East holding both ace and queen of spades, declarer was in a lose-lose position. He played low from dummy, but East won the queen and cashed the ace. Down one.

Deal 17

We have considered in detail the Attitude Signal and the Count Signal. The third - and last - basic signal is the Suit Preference Signal. As the name suggests, this signal directs partner to a particular suit: a low spot card calls for the lower-ranking other suit; a high card calls for the higher-ranking suit.

The message of the Suit Preference Signal (SPS) will potentially conflict with the other types of signal, so it is vital that the partnership know which signal is being sent. The key is to remember that SPS is only effective when you cannot desire the suit which is actually being used for the signal.

The most important use for SPS is when leading a suit for partner to trump. Clearly you cannot be sending a message about the suit led

- because partner has none. Instead you are indicating to partner which other suit (ignoring trumps) you would like returned, with a view to winning a lead of that suit and giving partner another ruff.

Exercise: Hearts are trumps. You hold ♣A108642, win partner's ♣3 lead (clearly a singleton) with ♣A, and must return the right spot card for partner to ruff.

(i) You have ♦A.

(ii) You have ♠A.

Which club do you return in each case?

Answers:

(i) ♣2. Asks for the lower-ranking of the remaining suits, diamonds.

(ii) ♣10. Requesting the higher-ranking outside suit, spades.

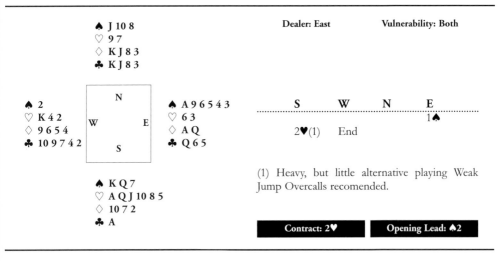

	♠ J 10 8	
	♡ 9 7	
	◇ K J 8 3	
	♣ K J 8 3	

♠ 2		♠ A 9 6 5 4 3
♡ K 4 2		♡ 6 3
◇ 9 6 5 4		◇ A Q
♣ 10 9 7 4 2		♣ Q 6 5

	♠ K Q 7	
	♡ A Q J 10 8 5	
	◇ 10 7 2	
	♣ A	

Dealer: East   Vulnerability: Both

S	W	N	E
			1♠
2♥(1)	End		

(1) Heavy, but little alternative playing Weak Jump Overcalls recomended.

Contract: 2♥   **Opening Lead: ♠2**

"Sorry, partner. We might have missed a game here", said declarer, as dummy was tabled in a lowly 2♥. The defence were soon to demonstrate that this comment was somewhat inaccurate.

East won West's two of spades lead, a likely singleton (he would lead top from two), and returned the nine of spades as a SPS for diamonds (higher-ranked than clubs). West

ruffed, and duly returned a diamond. East won the queen, cashed the ace (voiding himself), then led the seven of spades, another SPS for the higher-ranked diamonds.

West ruffed the third spade, returned a third diamond for East to ruff, whereupon a fourth spade ensured that West's now bare king of trumps had to score - via a Trump Promotion. Down two.

Deal 18

The Suit Preference Signal (SPS) is often referred to in this country as "McKenney", after a American Bridge columnist of the 1930s and 40s, William McKenney, who helped to publicise it. Its inventor, however, in 1934, was another American, Hy Lavinthal.

In Lavinthal's ingenious signal, a high spot card calls for the higher-ranking suit; a low spot card calls for the lower-ranking suit. Note that normally there will only be two possible suits in the game, with the suit used for the signal and trumps both eliminated.

The most common use for SPS is leading a suit for partner to trump. However, if the attitude (like/dislike), and count (suit length), is known (or irrelevant), SPS can be used in other situations. Here are two:

(a) Indicating where you have an entry, useful in notrumps when you have established a suit.

(b) When dummy has no losers in the suit partner has led (in a trump contract), making a continuation implausible.

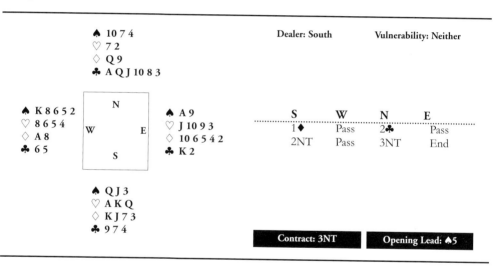

N			
♠ 10 7 4		Dealer: South	Vulnerability: Neither
♡ 7 2			
◇ Q 9			
♣ A Q J 10 8 3			

West hand: ♠ K 8 6 5 2 ♡ 8 6 5 4 ◇ A 8 ♣ 6 5

East hand: ♠ A 9 ♡ J 10 9 3 ◇ 10 6 5 4 2 ♣ K 2

South hand: ♠ Q J 3 ♡ A K Q ◇ K J 7 3 ♣ 9 7 4

S	W	N	E
1◇	Pass	2♣	Pass
2NT	Pass	3NT	End

Contract: 3NT   **Opening Lead: ♠5**

This deal, illustrating point (a) above, sees West lead the five of spades to 3NT. East wins the ace, returns a second spade to declarer's jack, and West wins the king.

West is going to concede a third spade to declarer, but it is vital to show partner where his entry lies. He can do this by returning a low spade, as a SPS for the lower ranking outside suit. Clearly (looking at dummy) clubs are out of the picture, so West is flagging for diamonds in preference to hearts.

Declarer wins West's two of spades, and runs the nine of clubs. The finesse loses, East winning the king. The big question for East is: how to reach his partner's hand and the established spade winners?

Without the signal, East might well be tempted to switch to hearts - after all, declarer opened One Diamond, dummy is weaker in hearts, and East has an alluring jack-ten-nine sequence in hearts. As you will note, a heart switch from East would be disastrous, declarer able to win, and run nine tricks via five clubs, three hearts and a spade.

The SPS signal told East to switch to diamonds, however, and the game contract is soon defeated. West wins East's diamond with the ace, and cashes his two long spades. Down two.

Deal 19

The Suit Preference Signal, in which a low card calls for the lower ranking other suit, and a high card calls for the higher-ranking other suit, should come with a government health warning.

The SPS should only be used when the signal suit is not a possible next play. For example a spade signal should only be interpreted as Suit Preference (rather than the much more common Attitude or Count) if it is implausible for a spade to be led to the following trick. This will be the case if:

(i) Partner is known to be out of the signal suit (now / after the trick). Perhaps you are giving partner a ruff, or clearing the suit in notrumps. In each case you can indicate where your side entry lies.

(ii) Dummy has no losers in the suit led (i.e. a singleton / only winners); a continuation is unlikely.

Exercise: Diamonds are trumps. Which suit is partner requesting?

	Dummy	
You	♥4(singleton)	*Partner*
lead		(i) ♥3
♥A		(ii) ♥9

(i) Clubs (low card = lower suit).
(ii) Spades (high card = higher suit).

Note that if you want a trump (or a heart continuation), play a middle card.

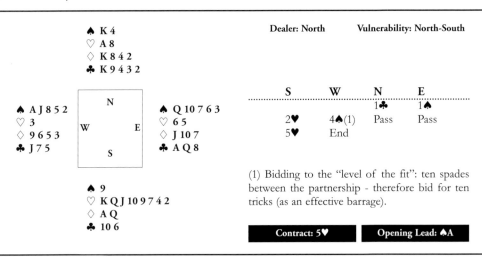

	♠ K 4		
	♡ A 8		
	◇ K 8 4 2		
	♣ K 9 4 3 2		

Dealer: North   **Vulnerability: North-South**

West hand: ♠ A J 8 5 2 ♡ 3 ◇ 9 6 5 3 ♣ J 7 5

East hand: ♠ Q 10 7 6 3 ♡ 6 5 ◇ J 10 7 ♣ A Q 8

South hand: ♠ 9 ♡ K Q J 10 9 7 4 2 ◇ A Q ♣ 10 6

S	W	N	E
		1♣	1♠
2♥	4♠(1)	Pass	Pass
5♥	End		

(1) Bidding to the "level of the fit": ten spades between the partnership - therefore bid for ten tricks (as an effective barrage).

Contract: 5♥	**Opening Lead: ♠A**

On our illustrative deal West pushed South to the Five-level, and led the ace of spades. A look at dummy's no-loser spades made it clear that a spade continuation was out of the question. East's spade card was therefore a SPS.

Wanting a club as opposed to a diamond (otherwise West would be guessing blindly), East signalled with his lowest spade, the three. West now knew to switch to a club at Trick Two, and East could beat dummy's king with the ace and cash the queen. Down one.

Footnote: let me return to my original theme: that the SPS comes with a government health warning. I see it (over)used in totally inappropriate circumstances (including as a discarding method - more on this anon). If you feel uneasy about the SPS, I would recommend restricting its use to those situations in which you are giving partner a ruff (the most common scenario).

Deal 20

At the half-way point in the book, it is fitting to summarise the three basic defensive signals:

(A). *Attitude - Like/Dislike: "Throw low means no, throw high means aye".* This is the most common and important signal - by far. Use when partner is leading, on the first round of a suit, to tell them whether or not you want a continuation.

(B). *Count - Suit Length: "HELO" - High=Even number; Low=Odd Number.* Use when declarer is leading, and partner needs to know how many cards you (therefore declarer) holds.

(C). *Suit Preference - a request for the lower/higher ranking other suit.* A low card calls for the lower ranking, and a high card calls for the higher-ranking. Use when leading a suit for partner to trump.

There is one aspect that is common to all three: it is the RELATIVE size of the card, as opposed to the absolute value, that is important. A two, three, or four is probably low; a seven, eight or nine is probably high. However this need not be the case.

Take these attitude situations:

	Dummy	
Partner	♦654	*You*
♦A led		(i) ♦Q32
		(ii) ♦987

In (i), you wish to encourage, but the best you can do is ♦3.

In (ii), you wish to discourage, but can play only ♦7.

Clearly these examples are somewhat contrived - but they make the key point: that "high" and "low" are relative.

Is there any hope that partner will be able to interpret them correctly?

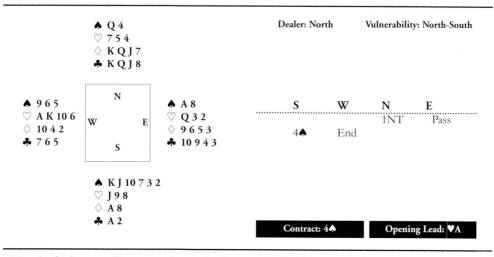

	♠ Q 4	
	♡ 7 5 4	
	◇ K Q J 7	
	♣ K Q J 8	

Dealer: North   Vulnerability: North-South

♠ 9 6 5	N	♠ A 8
♡ A K 10 6	W E	♡ Q 3 2
◇ 10 4 2		◇ 9 6 5 3
♣ 7 6 5	S	♣ 10 9 4 3

S	W	N	E
		1NT	Pass
4♠	End		

	♠ K J 10 7 3 2
	♡ J 9 8
	◇ A 8
	♣ A 2

Contract: 4♠	**Opening Lead: ♥A**

West leads the ace of hearts, and sees the first trick go ♥4, ♥3, ♥8. His first reaction is surely that his partner has discouraged ("throw low means no"). But something has been overlooked.

Where is the two?

Unless South is falsecarding, East has the two.

[NB: take note declarers: play the eight from ♥Q82.] West should not try to guess his partner's ace, in the hope of receiving a second heart lead through declarer. Rather he should cash the king of hearts, lead over to his partners queen (or ruff, if he held ♥32), and see him score his ace. Down one.

Deal 21

If you encourage partner's lead ("throw high means aye"), he will play another round; if you discourage partner's lead ("throw low means no"), he will make the "Obvious Switch".

Though the above points are hardly earth-shattering, there are important logical repercussions:

(a) If you are desperate for the Obvious Switch, then you should discourage the lead, even if you quite like it.

(b) If you desperately do not want the Obvious Switch, then you should encourage the lead, even if you do not much like it.

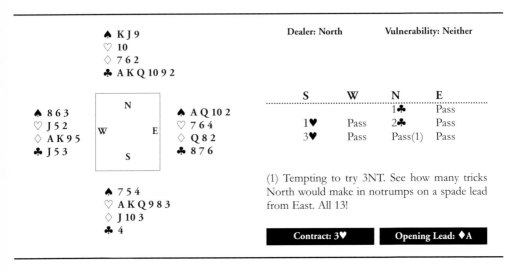

	♠ K J 9
	♡ 10
	◊ 7 6 2
	♣ A K Q 10 9 2

Dealer: North   **Vulnerability: Neither**

West:
♠ 8 6 3
♡ J 5 2
◊ A K 9 5
♣ J 5 3

East:
♠ A Q 10 2
♡ 7 6 4
◊ Q 8 2
♣ 8 7 6

South:
♠ 7 5 4
♡ A K Q 9 8 3
◊ J 10 3
♣ 4

S	W	N	E
		1♣	Pass
1♥	Pass	2♣	Pass
3♥	Pass	Pass(1)	Pass

(1) Tempting to try 3NT. See how many tricks North would make in notrumps on a spade lead from East. All 13!

Contract: 3♥   **Opening Lead: ◆A**

West led the ace of diamonds against 3♥. East held the equal honour (the queen), and would therefore normally encourage the lead.

Say East looks no further than at his diamond holding, signalling with the eight ("throw high means aye"). West obediently plays the king and a third diamond. East wins the queen, but can do no better than cash the ace of spades. Nine tricks - contract made.

Looking at dummy, the obvious switch for West to make is to spades - not dummy's long, strong clubs and not trumps. As East wants a spade switch from his partner even more than a diamond continuation, he should discourage the diamond lead.

East correctly signalled at Trick One with the two of diamonds ("throw low means no"). West duly switched to a spade at Trick Two, crucially through dummy's honours, and now the defence were in charge.

Declarer tried dummy's jack of spades, but East won cheaply with the queen, then reverted to diamonds, by playing the queen and a third round. West won his king, and a second spade soon followed.

East beat dummy's nine of spades with the ten, cashed the ace of spades felling dummy's king, and then came the Coup de Grace. East led the thirteenth spade. Whether or not declarer ruffed high (he elected not to), West's jack of trumps was promoted into a trick. Down three.

Deal 22

If you discourage partner's lead ("throw low means no"), partner is going to make the "Obvious Switch" (dummy's weakest suit). If you do not want the obvious shift, then it may well be right to encourage partner's lead, even if you are not mad about it. Take this deal.

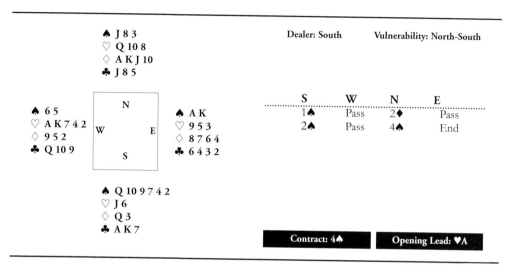

| ♠ J 8 3 |
| ♡ Q 10 8 |
| ◇ A K J 10 |
| ♣ J 8 5 |

Dealer: South   Vulnerability: North-South

	N	
♠ 6 5		♠ A K
♡ A K 7 4 2	W E	♡ 9 5 3
◇ 9 5 2		◇ 8 7 6 4
♣ Q 10 9	S	♣ 6 4 3 2

| ♠ Q 10 9 7 4 2 |
| ♡ J 6 |
| ◇ Q 3 |
| ♣ A K 7 |

S	W	N	E
1♠	Pass	2◇	Pass
2♠	Pass	4♠	End

| Contract: 4♠ | | Opening Lead: ♥A |

West led the ace of hearts, and, with no third round control (queen or doubleton), East was just about to discourage the suit ("throw low means no"). Had he done so, West would (should) have switched to clubs, dummy's weakness.

Disaster! On a club switch, declarer rises with dummy's jack, winning, then cashes three top diamonds, discarding his heart loser as both opponents follow. He then knocks out the ace-king of trumps and claims his game (and rubber).

Although naming and shaming is totally antithetical to the way Bridge should be played, the above defensive disaster would be East's fault for his signal, not West's for failing to cash the king of hearts. Swap the king of spades for the two of spades and the king of clubs for the two of clubs, and switching to a club at Trick Two (without cashing the king of hearts), would be the only way to beat the game.

The important defensive principle is this: *when signalling, look further than your holding in the suit led. Ask yourself what you want partner to do next.*

On the deal in question, East looks further than his heart holding, when deciding whether or not to encourage a heart continuation. He reflects that, apart from hating the idea of the "obvious switch", clubs, he knows that the game will fail if West's second top heart cashes (and it rates to - if West held six hearts headed by the ace-king, he might well have overcalled the suit).

East plays the nine of hearts ("Throw high means aye") at Trick One (key play). West naturally continues with the king of hearts at Trick Two, then leads a third heart. He is expecting (from his partner's encouraging signal) that his partner will ruff a third heart. But he is soon to realise why he was asked to continue the suit, as East scores his ace-king of trumps to defeat the game. Down one.

Deal 23

Partner leads an ace (versus a trump contract), and dummy tables a doubleton. You also hold a doubleton - should you encourage the lead ("Throw high means aye") or not ("Throw low means no")?

The key question to ask is: "Do I want partner to continue the suit, leading the king and a third round?" (for this he will do if I encourage the lead). The crux will be whether or not you can (and want to) overruff dummy.

Exercise: Partner leads ♠A against a heart contract. Do you encourage the spade lead?

	Dummy	
Partner	♠107	*You*
♠A led	♥QJ3	♠94
		(i) ♥K52
		(ii) ♥974
		(iii)♥10987

In (i) you should encourage (signalling with ♠9). Partner will play ♠K and a third round, whereupon you will overruff dummy's ♥J with ♥K, and so score a trick with a card that would likely not have made (declarer finessing).

In (ii) you should discourage (♠4), because you cannot overruff dummy. [I am assuming that you can cope with the Obvious Switch, for that is where partner will undoubtedly turn at Trick Two.]

In (iii) you cannot overruff dummy, but a third round of trumps will create a Trump Promotion for you. If dummy ruffs low, you can overruff; if dummy ruffs with ♥J/♥Q, you can discard, and score a fourth-round trump. Signal with ♠9.

	♠ A Q 7 6	
	♡ J 3	
	◇ J 7	
	♣ K Q 9 6 3	
♠ 10 5 4 2	**N**	♠ J 9 8
♡ 6	**W E**	♡ 10 9 8 2
◇ A K 8 6		◇ 9 3 2
♣ A 10 7 2	**S**	♣ J 5 4
	♠ K 3	
	♡ A K Q 7 5 4	
	◇ Q 10 5 4	
	♣ 8	

Dealer: North   Vulnerability: East-West

S	W	N	E
		1♣	Pass
1♥	Pass	1♠	Pass
2♦(1)	Pass	2♥(2)	Pass
4♥	End		

(1) Fourth Suit Forcing - "We're going to game - more information please".
(2) Having already shown his five-four black-suit shape, and with no stopper in the fourth suit, North returns to responder's first suit with his honour-doubleton.

Contract: 4♥	**Opening Lead: ♦A**

East went one step further. He feigned a doubleton diamond by playing the nine on West's ace lead, so that (a) partner would continue (he certainly didn't want any other suit led), and (b) dummy would ruff the third round high, promoting a trump trick for the Machiavellian defender.

West played a crucial role too, cashing the ace of clubs (after the ace-king of diamonds) before leading the third diamond. Declarer ruffed with the jack, scowled when East followed, crossed to the ace-king-queen of hearts, and was shortly writing down -50, East scoring a fourth-round trump trick. Down one.

Deal 24

Discarding means throwing away when you cannot follow to the suit led. You have twin goals:

(a) *Telling partner which suit you like (and want led).*
(b) *Keeping the right cards, to avoid declarer making more than his due.*

Focusing first on (a), there are several discarding methods on the market, including Dodds, Revolving and McKenney (Suit Preference). These are all similar in nature. Take McKenney: say partner is running spade winners versus a notrump contract. A low diamond discard would call for a club; a high diamond discard would call for a heart.

Here are some reasons why I will NOT be recommending an artificial system such as those above, preferring a natural, attitude-based approach:

(i) A natural method is easier to remember, and put into practice.

(ii) What do you do when you cannot spare (or do not have) the right spot cards to send the (say) McKenney message? A natural method is more flexible.

(iii) Is your (say) McKenney discard a command, or merely a suggestion? A natural method enables you to both suggest and command.

I won't give more reasons, but will say that you'll struggle to find a top-level pair playing the above artificial methods. So breathe a sigh of relief (I hope!) - we are going to play a simple, attitude-based discarding style, in which signalling through discards is just like signalling when following suit.

> *"Throw high means aye*
> *Throw low means no".*

If you want a particular suit to be led, you throw away a high card in that suit (assuming you can afford to). This is the most clear-cut, simple-to-read, way of attracting partner's attention to a particular suit.

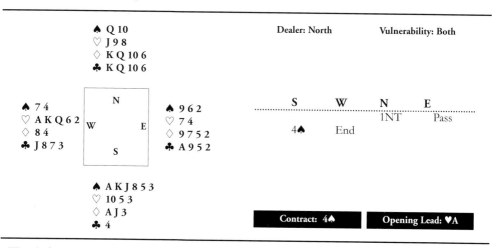

Dealer: North   Vulnerability: Both

S	W	N	E
		1NT	Pass
4♠	End		

Contract: 4♠   **Opening Lead: ♥A**

West led the ace of hearts against 4♠. You as East encourage (holding third-round control), and this tells West (who knows that your third-round control is a doubleton not the queen), that declarer has three hearts. He cashes the ace-king-queen of hearts, and you have to find a discard. What could be easier than the nine of clubs - "throw high means aye". West promptly switches to a club, and your cashing ace ensures down one.

Footnote: Playing with a drowsy partner, an alternative would be to trump partner's winning third heart, and cash the ace of clubs!

Deal 25

I am teaching you a simple, natural discarding style, in which signalling through discards is just like signalling when following suit.

> **"Throw high means aye**
> **Throw low means no".**

If you want a particular suit to be led, you throw away a high card in that suit (assuming you can afford to). This is the most clear-cut, simple-to-read, way of attracting partner's attention to a particular suit.

However if you cannot afford to release a high card for fear of costing a trick (and this will be especially true in notrumps), then throw away a low card of another suit, relying on partner to work out what you do want. This illustrative example may be somewhat contrived, but I hope it makes the point.

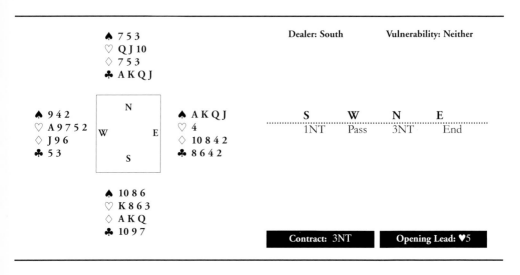

	♠ 7 5 3	
	♡ Q J 10	
	◇ 7 5 3	
	♣ A K Q J	

Dealer: South — Vulnerability: Neither

♠ 9 4 2	N	♠ A K Q J
♡ A 9 7 5 2	W E	♡ 4
◇ J 9 6		◇ 10 8 4 2
♣ 5 3	S	♣ 8 6 4 2

	♠ 10 8 6	
	♡ K 8 6 3	
	◇ A K Q	
	♣ 10 9 7	

S	W	N	E
1NT	Pass	3NT	End

Contract: 3NT   **Opening Lead:** ♥5

West leads the five of hearts against 3NT, and declarer wins in dummy. Needing a second trick from hearts, declarer leads a heart straight back at Trick Two. This is far better tactics than cashing the top tricks in the minors first, making it blindingly obvious to the defenders that they need to switch to spades (as well as setting up defensive long card(s) in those suits).

The crunch has arrived: what should you as East discard at Trick Two. Clearly desperate for a spade, you cannot release a high spade for you need all four of your spades to win tricks in order to defeat the game. You therefore need to throw low in a suit you don't want, and hope that your partner can work out to switch to spades. But which minor-suit deuce (two) should you discard?

The key point is this: your partner is looking at dummy and is never going to switch to clubs; throw a low club and you are not telling him anything he didn't already know. Partner is purely deciding whether to switch to spades or diamonds. If you put him off one of those suits (by throwing away a low card in it) he will surely lead the other.

East correctly discarded the two of diamonds ("throw low means no"), and West had only one place to go: spades. East won the spade switch, and promptly cashed his other three winners. Down one.

Deal 26

You can send messages to partner when you discard (throw away), in the normal "attitude" fashion. I.e.

**"Throw high means aye
Throw low means no".**

This scheme has the merit of simplicity; it also has the merit of flexibility. For you can throw high in a suit you want; or low in a suit you don't want.

Sending a message that is specifically related to the suit you are throwing feels a much more intuitive approach than those who prefer artificial discarding methods (such as McKenney or Revolving) where the message relates to a different suit. I hope you agree.

Bear in mind that only the first discard within a given suit sends a message; and the first discard of all sends the strongest message - by far.

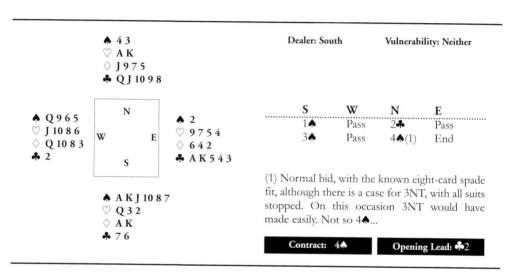

Dealer: South   Vulnerability: Neither

♠ 4 3
♡ A K
◇ J 9 7 5
♣ Q J 10 9 8

♠ Q 9 6 5
♡ J 10 8 6
◇ Q 10 8 3
♣ 2

♠ 2
♡ 9 7 5 4
◇ 6 4 2
♣ A K 5 4 3

♠ A K J 10 8 7
♡ Q 3 2
◇ A K
♣ 7 6

S	W	N	E
1♠	Pass	2♣	Pass
3♠	Pass	4♠(1)	End

(1) Normal bid, with the known eight-card spade fit, although there is a case for 3NT, with all suits stopped. On this occasion 3NT would have made easily. Not so 4♠...

Contract: 4♠   **Opening Lead: ♣2**

West led the two of clubs against 4♠, and East could clearly read this as a singleton: West would not lead dummy's bid suit without a good reason, and in any event would have led top from two cards. He won Trick One with the king, then cashed the ace. What should West discard?

West wants a third club, but must realise that a diamond switch will look appealing to East. West could hold:

♠ 7 6 5 2
♡ 10 8 6 2
◇ A Q 10 3
♣ 2

West must put his partner off the diamond switch, by discarding a low card of the suit.

With a heart switch inconceivable (looking at dummy), East will now be bound to play a third club. Though he knows declarer is out of clubs, there is promise of a Trump Promotion, as partner, also void of clubs, plays afterwards.

Declarer ruffs with the jack, and West, observing the maxim *"do not overruff with a trump that will win a trick anyway - and you might win a second trump trick"*, discards (a diamond).

Overruff with the queen, and that would be West's last trump trick. Discard, and declarer is bound to fail, crossing to dummy in hearts to play a trump to the ten. West takes his queen and waits to score the promoted nine. Down one.

Deal 27

One discard from partner can make all the difference to your defence. So if you have a choice, delay taking a winner until you have given partner a chance to make that all-important first discard. This deal is a case in point.

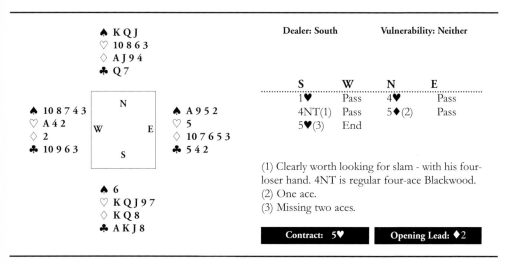

```
              ♠ K Q J
              ♡ 10 8 6 3
              ◇ A J 9 4
              ♣ Q 7
                      N
♠ 10 8 7 4 3                      ♠ A 9 5 2
♡ A 4 2      W        E           ♡ 5
◇ 2                               ◇ 10 7 6 5 3
♣ 10 9 6 3           S            ♣ 5 4 2

              ♠ 6
              ♡ K Q J 9 7
              ◇ K Q 8
              ♣ A K J 8
```

Dealer: South   **Vulnerability: Neither**

S	W	N	E
1♥	Pass	4♥	Pass
4NT(1)	Pass	5◇(2)	Pass
5♥(3)	End		

(1) Clearly worth looking for slam - with his four-loser hand. 4NT is regular four-ace Blackwood.
(2) One ace.
(3) Missing two aces.

Contract: 5♥	Opening Lead: ◆2

Question: Why was West confident of beating 5♥, even though his opponents had tried for slam via Blackwood?

Answer: The whole raison d'etre of the Blackwood convention (whether normal four-ace, or Roman Key Card) is to avoid bidding to slam when missing two aces. South's sign-off in 5♥ is indicative that East-West hold two aces. West's partner therefore holds an ace.

A promising defence suggests itself. West leads his singleton diamond; on winning his ace of trumps, he puts partner on play with his ace, and receives a second diamond for a ruff. Down one.

To the table. West led his singleton diamond, declarer winning in hand and leading the king of trumps. West took the ace and...

Not so fast, not so fast! West does not know which black ace his partner holds, the vital entry for his second-round diamond ruff. He needs to duck his ace of trumps for a round (key play).

Playing low on the king of trumps, therefore, and winning a second trump with the ace, West was able to view his partner's discard (declarer's strong bidding suggested that he would have five trumps, leaving East with just a singleton).

East threw the nine of spades - "throw high means aye" - and now West was in no doubt as to what to do. He switched to a spade. East won the ace, and a second diamond brought the desired result: West ruffed for down one.

Perhaps West should have doubled?

Deal 28

When discarding (throwing away when you cannot follow suit), you have two jobs:

(a) **Sending the right message to partner.** This is usually of primary importance when partner is on lead, with the first discard sending the strongest message. Use the familiar attitude maxim: "Throw high means aye, throw low means no".

(b) **Keeping the right cards.** This is usually the more important of the two jobs when declarer is on lead, and also after your first attitude-based discard.

Remember those Trick 12 situations where you have to "guess" which of your two remaining cards to keep, and which to discard. Ultimately there is no substitute for accurate counting (sorry!); but there are some good tips to help you and partner earlier in the defence.

Perhaps the most important such tip is to *"keep equal length with dummy"* - provided your highest card is higher than dummy's lowest card. Take this striking example.

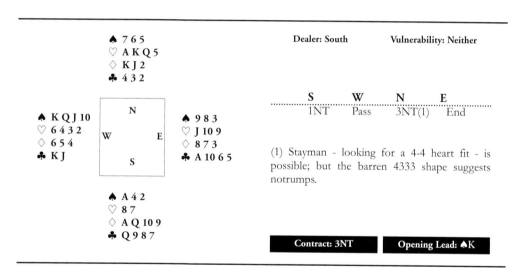

♠ 7 6 5
♡ A K Q 5
◇ K J 2
♣ 4 3 2

♠ K Q J 10
♡ 6 4 3 2
◇ 6 5 4
♣ K J

♠ 9 8 3
♡ J 10 9
◇ 8 7 3
♣ A 10 6 5

♠ A 4 2
♡ 8 7
◇ A Q 10 9
♣ Q 9 8 7

Dealer: South   Vulnerability: Neither

S	W	N	E
1NT	Pass	3NT(1)	End

(1) Stayman - looking for a 4-4 heart fit - is possible; but the barren 4333 shape suggests notrumps.

Contract: 3NT   **Opening Lead: ♠K**

West leads the king of spades against 3NT, declarer ducking once, and winning the second round (not ducking again, for fear of a club switch, and three fast losers in that suit). He then rattled off his four diamond winners.

West followed to three diamonds, but needed to discard on the fourth. Neither back suit looked an appealing discard - with two spade winners and the king of clubs that needed protecting. It looked all-too-easy to discard a "useless" heart.

However to throw away a heart was the one thing West could NOT afford to do, for he needed to keep equal length with dummy's hearts (his highest heart, the six, beating dummy's lowest heart, the five).

Either a spade or a club could be spared, and West (eventually) passed the test, letting go a spade winner. All declarer could do was to cash the ace-king-queen of hearts and, with West's six of hearts beating dummy's five, concede the remainder. Down one.

Deal 29

The following tips will help, when deciding which cards to keep, and which to let go.

(i) Keep suits that partner is throwing.

(ii) Keep suits in which partner is known to have fewer cards.

(iii) Keep equal length with dummy.

(iv) Keep four-card lengths.

All common-sense stuff, I hope you'll agree.

Take point (iv). By far the most common hand pattern - therefore suit pattern around the table - is 4-4-3-2. If declarer/dummy has a four-card length, then, subject to the size of the cards, the defender with the four-card holding must retain his length, whilst the defender with the shorter length can freely discard from the suit.

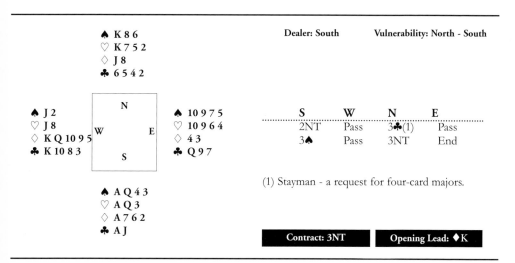

```
            ♠ K 8 6
            ♡ K 7 5 2
            ◇ J 8
            ♣ 6 5 4 2
♠ J 2              N              ♠ 10 9 7 5
♡ J 8                             ♡ 10 9 6 4
◇ K Q 10 9 5  W       E          ◇ 4 3
♣ K 10 8 3         S              ♣ Q 9 7
            ♠ A Q 4 3
            ♡ A Q 3
            ◇ A 7 6 2
            ♣ A J
```

Dealer: South   **Vulnerability: North - South**

S	W	N	E
2NT	Pass	3♣(1)	Pass
3♠	Pass	3NT	End

(1) Stayman - a request for four-card majors.

| **Contract: 3NT** | **Opening Lead: ◆K** |

West leads the king of diamonds against 3NT and, pleased to see the jack in the short holding in dummy, continues with the queen, pinning that jack. Declarer ducks his ace twice, but wins West's ten of diamonds continuation, with dummy throwing a spade. Not before East has to make a discard, however. What should he throw?

Although it looks tempting to keep a guard (i.e. two low cards) for his only picture card, the queen of clubs, in fact clubs is the only suit from which he can safely discard. The bidding has told East that declarer holds four spades; a look at dummy reveals four hearts. East must retain equal length with both these suits [see points (ii), (iii) and (iv)]. Throw a spade, and declarer has a fourth spade trick; throw a heart and dummy has a fourth heart trick. Only a club can be spared.

At the table, East correctly (although understandably reluctantly) let go the seven of clubs, and now declarer went down, trying one major-suit then the other in the hope that the six missing cards would split 3-3, and all fall under his three top cards. No good - East held the fourth-round winner in both, and declarer was soon writing 100 points above the line in the "They" column. Down one.

Deal 30

As a general principle, your first discard will send a message to partner - "Throw high means aye; throw low means no". Subsequent discards are more concerned with letting go what you don't need, and retaining what you do need. Here are some guidelines:

(A). *Keep equal length with dummy (and declarer - if you can deduce how many cards he holds)*. Particularly important when dummy has specifically four cards, be very reluctant to discard from four cards down to three unless:

(i) all of dummy's cards are higher than yours.

Or

(ii) you think partner also has four cards, enabling him to guard the suit.

Or

(iii) you have to keep another suit that is even more valuable.

(B). *Throw from long, weak suits*.

(i) Don't bother to keep length winners in a trump contract - they will rarely make tricks (unless declarer is running out of trumps).

(ii) Don't keep length winners - even in notrumps - if you have no entry card.

(iii) As a rough guide, it is better to throw from a five-card suit than a three-card suit; but better to discard from a three-card suit than a four-card suit.

(C). *Plan your discards*.

If dummy is running a long suit, you know how many discards you will have to make. Do your thinking at the beginning, and try to discard in an order (and tempo) that will be as unhelpful as possible to declarer. If you take undue time, declarer will deduce that you have the key card(s). [NB: you cannot pause with nothing to think about - to deliberately mislead].

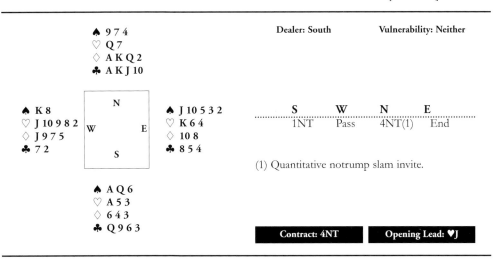

Dealer: South   Vulnerability: Neither

	S	W	N	E
	1NT	Pass	4NT(1)	End

(1) Quantitative notrump slam invite.

Contract: 4NT   Opening Lead: ♥J

You as West lead the jack of hearts, and are pleased when Trick One goes queen, king, low. Declarer ducks the heart continuation, and wins the third heart with his ace. He then rattles off four club tricks. What are your two discards?

Declarer is about to test diamonds. If you have thrown one, dummy's fourth card will be promoted. But if you have released both remaining hearts, declarer can then exit with the fourth diamond, forcing a lead away from your spade holding.

You must, in either order, discard one heart and, crucially (and as painlessly as possible), the eight of spades. After testing diamonds, declarer is likely to finesse the queen of spades, hoping your remaining spade is not the king. Down two.

Deal 31

Say you have to make discard(s). Here are some DOs and DONTs when deciding which suits to keep and which to release.

DON'T THROW when...
- It is equal length with dummy (or declarer).
- It is a four-card holding, unless you are sure declarer and dummy both have fewer cards.
- Partner is releasing the suit. He wants you to guard it.
- You are voiding yourself in a key suit. One round will see you show out, exposing partner's holding.

DO THROW when...
- Partner is guarding the suit.
- Your highest card is lower than dummy's lowest card.
- You are baring an honour in order to keep essential guards and/or winners elsewhere.
- It is dummy's short suit (in a trump contract), and declarer has spurned a chance to ruff losers (he cannot have any losers to ruff).

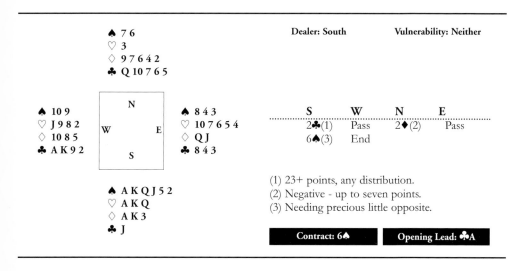

Dealer: South   Vulnerability: Neither

	♠ 7 6
	♡ 3
	◇ 9 7 6 4 2
	♣ Q 10 7 6 5

♠ 10 9		♠ 8 4 3
♡ J 9 8 2	N	♡ 10 7 6 5 4
◇ 10 8 5	W E	◇ Q J
♣ A K 9 2	S	♣ 8 4 3

| ♠ A K Q J 5 2 |
| ♡ A K Q |
| ◇ A K 3 |
| ♣ J |

S	W	N	E
2♣(1)	Pass	2♦(2)	Pass
6♠(3)	End		

(1) 23+ points, any distribution.
(2) Negative - up to seven points.
(3) Needing precious little opposite.

Contract: 6♠   **Opening Lead: ♣A**

You as West lead the ace of clubs, partner giving you a discouraging signal (the three) and declarer playing the jack. It is clear partner has three small cards, and declarer's jack is singleton (he would be mad to bid to slam with two club losers). You switch at Trick Two to the ten of trumps, passive, with the possibility of cutting down heart ruffs in dummy.

Declarer wins the trump switch, and rattles off five more trumps. You follow once, but must make four discards. What are they?

Because declarer has not bothered to ruff any hearts in dummy, he must have no losers in the suit. Throw away all your hearts (an occasion where you can void yourself - as the suit is irrelevant) Partner helpfully throws both his remaining clubs, to clarify the position.

Declarer then cashes his three top hearts. What do you release now? You know that declarer has no more clubs, and has no way to reach dummy. Therefore you can release all your clubs (yes - even the master king).

What you cannot afford to let go is a single diamond. Provided your last three cards are ♦1085, you will defeat the slam. Declarer, holding ♦AK5, will cash the ace-king (felling East's queen-jack), then give you the ten. Down one.

Deal 32

Bridge is a partnership game. You should always be on the look-out to tell partner as much as declarer knows.

Take this suit (in notrumps):

	Dummy	
Partner	♥75	*You*
♥8		♥QJ1094
	Declarer	
	♥AK632	

Declarer leads out the ace, all following low, and then follows with the king. Partner discards and you follow with...

Play the queen. This will put partner in the same position as declarer - both knowing that the suit is a dead loss for declarer and that (provided partner can read the suit lengths) you have three winners. Note that it costs you nothing to clue partner in.

When discarding, too, it is important to give as much information to partner as you can. Take this deal.

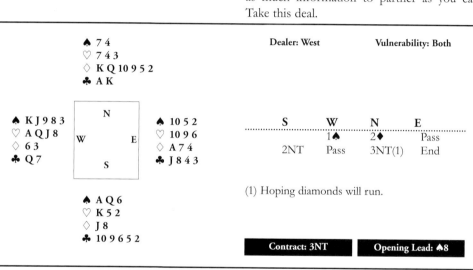

	♠ 7 4	
	♡ 7 4 3	
	◇ K Q 10 9 5 2	
	♣ A K	

Dealer: West   Vulnerability: Both

♠ K J 9 8 3	N	♠ 10 5 2
♡ A Q J 8	W E	♡ 10 9 6
◇ 6 3		◇ A 7 4
♣ Q 7	S	♣ J 8 4 3

S	W	N	E
	1♠	2◆	Pass
2NT	Pass	3NT(1)	End

♠ A Q 6
♡ K 5 2
◇ J 8
♣ 10 9 6 5 2

(1) Hoping diamonds will run.

Contract: 3NT	**Opening Lead: ♠8**

West led the eight of spades, to East's ten and declarer's queen. Declarer led the jack of diamonds, and a second diamond to dummy's nine. East correctly ducked his ace twice. By delaying winning until the third round, he would, crucially, receive a discard from West.

West: what should you throw on the third diamond - in order to give partner as much information as possible?

West is clearly desperate for a heart switch, but knows, all things being equal, that his partner is going to return a spade. For he opened One Spade, and led a spade. How to put partner off?

Arguably a low spade discard would do the job ("throw low means no"), but West did better. He discarded the king of spades! Such

dramatic discards have been termed "Alarm Clock", because they wake partner up. Let us see why this discard is so clever.

West would throw the most revealing card he can afford, so he must be denying the ace of spades (if he could throw the king, he could throw the ace). East could now count declarer with nine tricks in three suits (ace-queen of spades, plus, visible in dummy, five diamonds and the two top clubs).

When a defender can count declarer with nine tricks in three suits, the only chance of beating 3NT is to switch to the fourth suit, here hearts. East switched to the ten of hearts. A forlorn declarer ducked, and covered the nine with the king. But West took his ace, and cashed the queen-jack. Down one.

Deal 33

Let us consider the dreaded two-card guess. At Trick 12 you must keep one card, and let go of the other.

Clearly there is no substitute for some earlier counting, but...

(a) no one is perfect

(b) sometimes you simply cannot know which way to go. If you know that your partner is about to face such a dilemma, see whether you can help.

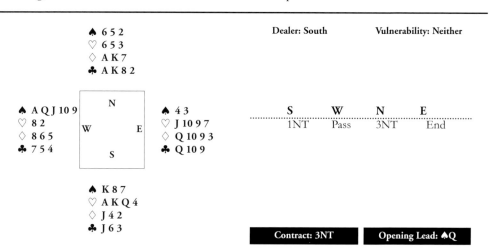

Dealer: South   Vulnerability: Neither

S	W	N	E
1NT	Pass	3NT	End

Contract: 3NT   Opening Lead: ♠Q

West led the queen of spades, and declarer took the king (duck, and he might never make it). Hoping for an even heart split, declarer next led out his three top cards in the suit.

No good - West discarded a minor on the third (it was actually a diamond, but East later forgot). Declarer then tried to drop a doubleton queen in either minor, leading out both dummy's ace-kings. No queen fell, and things were looking bleak for him: no ninth trick in sight. In desperation, he exited with a second spade.

West perked up and promptly cashed all his spades. This was the position as he led his last spade, unusually just a two-card ending:

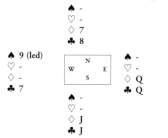

Which queen should East keep - and which could he afford to release? He did not know whether West's last card was a club or a diamond. Eventually he let go the queen of clubs. Declarer let go the jack of diamonds (which could now be of no use).

West then led his last card - a club - and an aghast East saw declarer win Trick 13 with his promoted jack of clubs. Nine tricks and game made.

Although East had made the more obvious mistake, throwing away the wrong queen at Trick 12, West was far more culpable. When declarer did not cash a ninth trick (before leading the second spade), he knew his partner held both minor-suit queens. He should not have cashed his last spade in the diagrammed position, instead leading the club. Then East would be bound to score the last two tricks with his minor-suit queens. Down one.

Deal 34

Back in 1963, Britain's I.G. Smith suggested the following ingenious signal, now almost universally played at top level (but rarely at club or social level).

The Smith Peter

In notrumps (only), on the first suit led by declarer, both defenders show whether they like the suit they led (within the context of what happened at Trick One). The standard approach, along familiar "high-aye, low-no" principles, is that an unnecessarily high spot card says, "I like the suit we led". A low card says, "I do not like the lead", and suggests a switch.

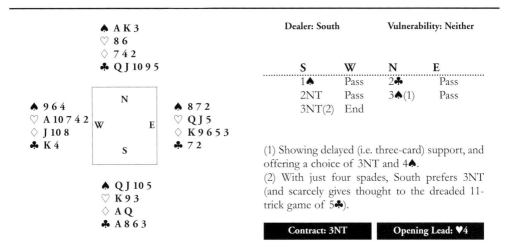

		♠ A K 3		
		♡ 8 6		
		◇ 7 4 2		
		♣ Q J 10 9 5		

♠ 9 6 4
♡ A 10 7 4 2
◇ J 10 8
♣ K 4

♠ 8 7 2
♡ Q J 5
◇ K 9 6 5 3
♣ 7 2

♠ Q J 10 5
♡ K 9 3
◇ A Q
♣ A 8 6 3

Dealer: South **Vulnerability: Neither**

S	W	N	E
1♠	Pass	2♣	Pass
2NT	Pass	3♠(1)	Pass
3NT(2)	End		

(1) Showing delayed (i.e. three-card) support, and offering a choice of 3NT and 4♠.
(2) With just four spades, South prefers 3NT (and scarcely gives thought to the dreaded 11-trick game of 5♣).

Contract: 3NT	**Opening Lead: ♥4**

You as West lead the four of hearts to East's jack and declarer's king. At Trick Two declarer crosses to the king of spades, in order to run the queen of clubs. You win the king and must decide on the next move. There are two viable alternatives:

(1). Play partner for the queen of hearts (perfectly possible - he would play the jack - cheaper - from queen-jack at Trick One). Lead a second (low) heart (although note that partner should unblock the queen if you lead the ace). Partner will win the hoped-for queen, and return a third heart to your winners.

(2). Play declarer for the queen of hearts (perfectly possible - declarer can choose which heart he wins with at Trick One). Switch to the jack of diamonds in the hope that partner holds the ace, and can win with the card to fire a second heart through declarer's remaining ♥Qx.

Both defences are entirely plausible, and the guess as to which course to pursue can only be resolved by using the Smith Peter.

If East holds his actual hand, he likes the heart lead (having the queen). He plays the eight of spades at Trick Two. West now knows to follow Line (1), continuing with hearts.

If, on the other hand, East holds, say,

♠ J 7 2
♡ J 5 3
◇ A 9 6 5 3
♣ 7 2

he follows with the two of spades at Trick Two: "I don't like your heart lead". West now knows to switch to diamonds (to East's ace), and receive a second heart, crucially through declarer's queen. Clever!

Deal 35

In our extensive look at defensive signalling, we have not yet mentioned what you can do in that special suit, trumps. Imagine this everyday scenario. You have three small trumps, the eight, the five and the three. Declarer is starting to draw them.

Question: Does the order you play your spot cards in the trump suit mean anything?

Answer: Yes. The standard approach* is to play that a high-low signal (i.e. eight first with 853) shows the desire/ability to ruff, usually with three trumps.

*Many modern experts now play Suit Preference Signals in trumps.

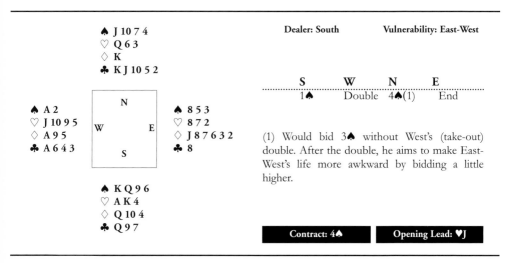

		♠ J 10 7 4				
		♡ Q 6 3				
		◇ K				
		♣ K J 10 5 2				

Dealer: South   **Vulnerability: East-West**

S	W	N	E
1♠	Double	4♠(1)	End

(1) Would bid 3♠ without West's (take-out) double. After the double, he aims to make East-West's life more awkward by bidding a little higher.

Contract: 4♠   **Opening Lead: ♥J**

You as West lead the jack of hearts, the first trick continuing three, two, ace. At Trick Two declarer leads the king of trumps. You win your ace, East following with the eight, and have to decide where to win the fourth defensive trick. Any ideas?

East has discouraged the heart lead (remember his two at Trick One), so declarer is marked with the king. Perhaps partner has the queen of clubs, and declarer will misguess, later leading to dummy's jack. Unlikely though: if he recalls your double, he will surely lead to the king. Is there anything else to play for?

Most certainly - and East's play of the eight of trumps has told you that it will work. His "hi-lo" trump signal (he has done the "hi" bit) has advertised the desire for a ruff. That can only be in clubs, so cash the ace of clubs and lead a second club (key plays). One further point: make the second club the two, as a Suit Preference Signal for the lower-ranked side-suit, diamonds.

East duly ruffs the second club and dutifully returns a diamond. You win the ace, whereupon a third club sees East ruff again. Down two.

You may now be reeling at all the different signals at your fingertips. Welcome to the world of expert Bridge, where every single free card by the defence means something!

Deal 36

As our book nears the end, it is important to return to basics. Answer the following:

(a) If you could take just one type of defensive signal to your desert island, which would it be?
(b) When is that signal used?
(c) How does it work?

Answers:

(a) The Attitude Signal.
(b) When partner leads; and when discarding.
(c) "Throw high means aye; throw low means no".

Signals are a huge help to defenders - as I'm sure you have realised; but only when combined with sensible Bridge-logic.

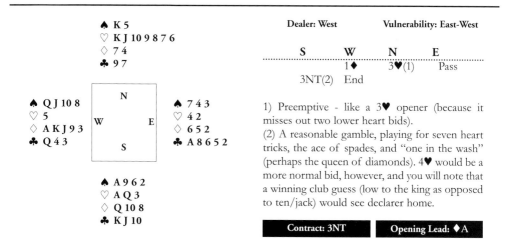

	♠ K 5
	♡ K J 10 9 8 7 6
	◇ 7 4
	♣ 9 7

Dealer: West   **Vulnerability: East-West**

S	W	N	E
	1◆	3♥(1)	Pass
3NT(2)	End		

1) Preemptive - like a 3♥ opener (because it misses out two lower heart bids).
(2) A reasonable gamble, playing for seven heart tricks, the ace of spades, and "one in the wash" (perhaps the queen of diamonds). 4♥ would be a more normal bid, however, and you will note that a winning club guess (low to the king as opposed to ten/jack) would see declarer home.

Contract: 3NT   **Opening Lead: ◆A**

You as West lead the ace of diamonds against 3NT (far better than the fourth highest nine: the queen might drop doubleton, plus you retain the lead). The first trick sees the four from dummy, the two from partner ("throw low means no"), and the eight from declarer.

With partner discouraging the diamond lead, the basic strategy is clear: put partner on play for a second diamond lead, crucially through declarer's queen. What is less clear is how to put partner in.

First of all, rule out hearts. For two reasons: (i) declarer's 3NT is surely based on a partial heart fit, and therefore the expectation of scoring seven heart tricks; (ii) if partner does hold the ace of hearts, he will always win the lead in time, as declarer is hardly going to make nine tricks without hearts.

Next consider spades: declarer would hardly bid 3NT without a stopper in the unbid major. If you switch to the (tempting, I admit) queen of spades, declarer will have nine tricks whenever he has the ace of spades and ♥Axx or better.

A club switch is by far the best. First of all, this is the most likely ace in partner's hand. But say partner has the king of clubs and the ace of spades: you will still survive, as declarer has just eight tricks.

On the actual layout, partner wins the club switch with the ace, whereupon a second diamond through declarer sees you beat the ten with the jack, cash the king felling the queen, and follow with the nine-three. Down two.

Deal 37

You must look beyond the end of your nose when deciding whether to signal "high means aye" or "low means no".

Rather than just looking at your holding in the suit partner led, you must ask yourself what you want partner to lead next. If you like the suit he has led, but want the "obvious switch" suit even more, then you should discourage partner from continuing.

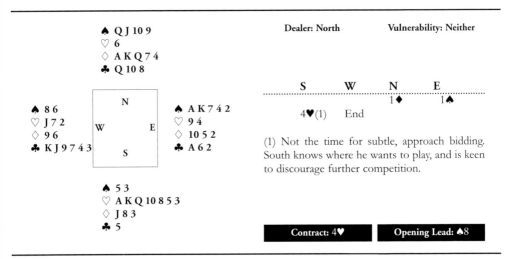

♠ Q J 10 9
♡ 6
◇ A K Q 7 4
♣ Q 10 8

♠ 8 6
♡ J 7 2
◇ 9 6
♣ K J 9 7 4 3

♠ A K 7 4 2
♡ 9 4
◇ 10 5 2
♣ A 6 2

♠ 5 3
♡ A K Q 10 8 5 3
◇ J 8 3
♣ 5

Dealer: North   Vulnerability: Neither

S	W	N	E
		1◇	1♠
4♥(1)	End		

(1) Not the time for subtle, approach bidding. South knows where he wants to play, and is keen to discourage further competition.

| Contract: 4♥ | Opening Lead: ♠8 |

West led the eight of spades against 4♥, his partner having overcalled the suit. East won the king, then cashed the ace. What next?

East could count that neither declarer, nor partner, held any more spades. A spade continuation was possible, as it might lead to a Trump Promotion (i.e. partner overtrumping declarer, or discarding if declarer trumped high). Equally possible was that two rounds of clubs would stand up, with partner holding the king, and declarer two small clubs.

There was one lead that catered to both above strategies: laying down the ace of clubs. West would then be able to signal, as appropriate.

Key moment. What is the correct signal from West on partner's ace of clubs?

West must look further than his king of clubs.

He should reason as follows:

"Encouraging a club continuation (by signalling with a high club) looks tempting; but declarer may not have a club left. What is 100% certain is that a third round of spades will promote a trump trick for my jack. Partner is bound to revert to spades if I put him off clubs, so discourage I must".

West signals with the three of clubs ("throw low means no"), and East reverts to the other plausible defence: a third spade.

Declarer's goose is now cooked. If he ruffs low (up to the ten), West overruffs with the jack. If he ruffs high, West discards, and waits to score his guarded jack on the third round of the suit. Down one.

Look out for the flip-side to this: when you don't like partner's lead, but want the obvious switch even less. Alternatively read the next deal!

Deal 38

In Bridge - unlike other games such as Poker - you are always involved, even with a bad hand.

This East held a truly terrible hand. Yet he was to play a key defensive role.

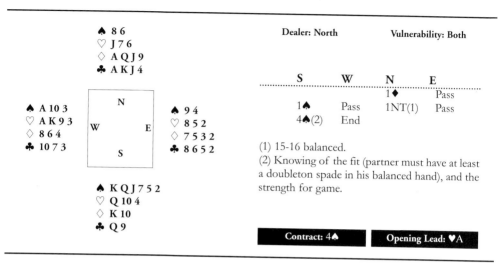

♠ 8 6
♡ J 7 6
◇ A Q J 9
♣ A K J 4

♠ A 10 3
♡ A K 9 3
◇ 8 6 4
♣ 10 7 3

N
W E
S

♠ 9 4
♡ 8 5 2
◇ 7 5 3 2
♣ 8 6 5 2

♠ K Q J 7 5 2
♡ Q 10 4
◇ K 10
♣ Q 9

Dealer: North   **Vulnerability: Both**

S	W	N	E
		1◇	Pass
1♠	Pass	1NT(1)	Pass
4♠(2)	End		

(1) 15-16 balanced.
(2) Knowing of the fit (partner must have at least a doubleton spade in his balanced hand), and the strength for game.

Contract: 4♠   **Opening Lead: ♥A**

West naturally kicked off with the ace of hearts against the 4♠ game: ace from ace-king is the best of all opening leads to a trump contract. Many Easts would just have played low, preparing themselves to do likewise for 13 tricks.

Not this East. Reasoning that he did not want his partner to switch suits, holding nothing in either minor, East signalled with the eight ("throw high means aye"). West naturally continued with the king and a third heart, and must have been a tad surprised when declarer won the third round with the queen, East following low again.

Over to declarer, who sought to lead the first round of trumps from dummy for two reasons.
(i) East might have a singleton ace, which would then "beat air".
(ii) East might have the ace of trumps and the last heart; even on a 3-2 trump split, beating a trump honour with the ace and leading the heart would create a trump promotion.

So declarer played a club to dummy, then led a trump from there.

West beat declarer's jack with the ace and, realising that East had encouraged hearts because he wanted a minor-suit switch even less, found the killing defence. Can you?

At Trick Six West led the thirteenth heart (key play). East ruffed with the crucial nine of trumps, and this forced declarer to overruff with the queen. He cashed the king of trumps, in the hope that the two remaining defensive trumps would fall one-one. But it was not to be. East discarded, and West's ten of trumps was promoted into a trick - the setting trick.

Declarer was down one - thanks to East's invaluable contribution. Instead of bemoaning his bad cards and losing interest, he made a clever encouraging signal at Trick One, because he wanted a switch even less. He then ruffed the fourth heart with his nine of trumps, the one card he held that was of any use, and so created the Trump Promotion.

Deal 39

The defence have made all the running in this book. Is declarer helpless, watching on as the defenders communicate vital information?

Actually, no. Declarer can often scramble the defensive signals.

Consider this classic layout:

(A)

	Dummy	
West	♥983	*East*
♥AK104		♥J75
	Declarer	
	♥Q62	

West leads the ace, East plays the five, and declarer...? If declarer woodenly follows with his lowest heart, the two, then West can read his partner's five as his lowest, and therefore a "throw low means no". If, however, declarer follows with the six (key "falsecard"), West

might well think that the layout is:

(B)

	Dummy	
West	♥983	*East*
♥AK104		♥Q52
	Declarer	
	♥J76	

Naturally declarer cannot afford to pause, or he gives the game away. So it is worth learning...

How to Scramble a Signal

If you want the opponents to continue the suit they have led (as in "A" above), you should encourage the lead yourself, as though you were the signaller (i.e. play the six from your ♥Q62). NB: You can only scramble a signal when you have a lower card.

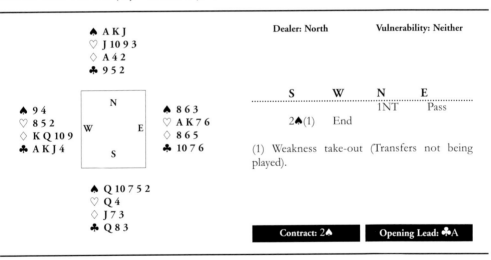

♠ A K J
♡ J 10 9 3
◇ A 4 2
♣ 9 5 2

♠ 9 4
♡ 8 5 2
◇ K Q 10 9
♣ A K J 4

♠ 8 6 3
♡ A K 7 6
◇ 8 6 5
♣ 10 7 6

♠ Q 10 7 5 2
♡ Q 4
◇ J 7 3
♣ Q 8 3

Dealer: North   **Vulnerability: Neither**

S	W	N	E
		1NT	Pass
2♠(1)	End		

(1) Weakness take-out (Transfers not being played).

Contract: 2♠   **Opening Lead: ♣A**

West led the ace of clubs against the 2♠ part-score. East tried to discourage a continuation by playing the six, but when declarer false-carded with the eight, West, thinking East held ♣Q63, continued with the king. East followed upwards with the seven, and West knew he'd been duped.

At Trick Three, West switched to the king of diamonds. Again East discouraged - with the

five; again South scrambled the signal by hiding his lower card, instead false-carding with the seven. Believing East to have ◆J53, West continued with the nine of diamonds. Fatally, for declarer ran the lead to his jack, drew trumps, and merely conceded two hearts.

Eight tricks and contract made, where down two was possible if West had not continued either minor.